Bread Machine

> Autorin: Ellen A. Harich

Contents

Fundamentals

The Recipes

Appendix

Irresistibly Aromatic and Crispy

With a bread machine and our tried and tested recipes, fresh bread is a luxury anyone can afford. Baking bread is easy and fun. Whether moist butter bread, sweet raisin bread, healthy whole-grain bread or a hearty country loaf, a bread machine lets you make the best bread in town. Once you get a taste, it's impossible to stop!

A bread machine can also assist you in making delicious bread and baked goods that you shape yourself. We'll show you how.

So enjoy yourself, and bon appetit!

Bread Machine Basics

Bread machines make baking bread easier than ever. Just place the ingredients in the bread pan, select the appropriate cycle and press "Start." In about three hours, you'll have a fresh loaf of home-made bread on the table.

Buying a bread machine

A variety of bread machines are available today, with different manufacturers usually offering several models. Prices typically range from $40 to $150. If you don't want to start out with a big investment, watch for sales (for example, from discounters). In our experience, even the inexpensive machines do the job.

Most bread machines feature nonstick and removable bread pans and dough hooks, and many come with measuring cups and spoons. In addition to their price, machines differ in the cycles available (Standard, White Bread, Quick, French, Dough, Whole Grain, etc.), cycle timing (for example, the Dough cycle can take 1 hour and 30 minutes or 2 hours and 25 minutes), the dimensions of the bread pan, the number of dough hooks (one or two), and the bread pan capacity.

The ideal loaf size is around 2 pounds. The recipes in this cookbook are based on models from different manufacturers, with loaves that weigh up to 2 pounds.

2 *The bread pan and dough hook are easily removed.*

Operation

Bread machines have a removable bread pan. To fill the pan, remove it from the machine and add the ingredients one at a time. Then return the pan to the machine, select the appropriate cycle, and after about three hours (time varies depending on the machine type), you can remove the finished loaf. If you want to knead the dough yourself or shape it by hand, then select the Dough cycle. The bread machine prepares the dough immediately and beeps to signal when it's time to remove the

1 *Fresh-baked bread looks delicious!*

dough and process it further. Bread machines also make great yeast dough for pizza.

Most machines have a timer function. You can, for example, fill the bread machine in the evening and set the timer so that fresh, warm bread will be ready to enjoy for breakfast. Not all breads can be baked with the timer function. This information is specified in each recipe in this book.

Touch test

During the kneading process, take an occasional peek inside the bread machine. This will give you an idea of the dough consistency. Poke the dough surface with your finger to test its elasticity. Dough that's dry makes firmer bread. Softer dough makes lighter bread. If it's too moist, however, the bread collapses.

It is therefore essential that you test the dough during its preparation because moisture levels in flours differ. Depending on their properties, you may need to add more water or flour to the dough. About 5–10 minutes into the first kneading phase, listen to the paddle. If the dough is too moist, the kneading paddle turns too fast, and you should add flour. If the dough is too dry, the kneading paddle is noisy, and you should add water. Add additional flour or water one tablespoon at a time, until the dough achieves optimal elasticity and shine.

Experiment!

Once you're confident using your bread machine, you can start creating your own personal specialty breads. For example, you can replace water with orange juice, apple juice or beer, or substitute kamut, millet, barley, amaranth, quinoa, etc., for small amounts of flour (typically no more than 2–4 ounces).

3 *The bread touch test is essential for checking consistency.*

Bread crusts

Today, almost all bread machines let you choose how light or dark your crust will be. A higher baking temperature results in a darker crust. Because each bread machine provides slightly different results, we can't make any general recommendation here. You'll just have to test it out on your own.

Basic Recipe

Before you start

Familiarize yourself with every aspect of your bread machine. Read the operating instructions carefully and note the manufacturer's directions on what to do before using the bread machine for the first time. Then set out everything you need to bake bread. A measuring cup for liquids and an accurate kitchen scale are essential.

Measuring flour

See Glossary on page 59.

White Bread

MAKES 1 LOAF

➤ 1½ cups water or milk
1½ tsp salt
16 oz (3¾ cups) unbleached all-purpose flour
1½ tsp dry yeast

🕙 Prep time: 10 minutes
Setting: White Bread (specific names of these settings vary by machine)
🕙 Timer: Yes

TIP Variations:
You can vary white bread dough in many different ways. Whenever you add an ingredient, remember: The dough's consistency must remain the same. For example, if you add moist ingredients (such as onions, herbs or bacon), you'll also need to add a little flour.

> **1** *Measure liquid. Sift and weigh flour. Sifted flour is lighter and mixes better. Measure out salt and yeast.*

> **2** *First add the liquid to the bread pan, then salt, flour, and yeast, in that order. Follow the operating instructions for your machine.*

> **3** *Remove the bread pan from the machine. After 10 minutes, turn the loaf out onto a rack. Let it cool before slicing.*

> **4** *White bread dough be varied in a variet ways: With bread se sonings (described page 9), smoked ba sautéed onions, he and seeds. For more information, see the*

Leavening Agents

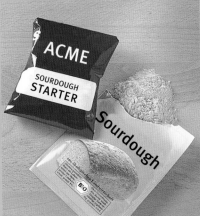

east: Both fresh compressed
d instant dry yeast are available.
mpared to fresh compressed
ast, dry yeast is easier to use, is
ss expensive and can be frozen
r longer periods of time. This
akes dry yeast ideal for bread
achines. Instant yeast is often
beled "bread machine yeast."
vo tablespoons instant yeast
quals 1 tablespoon fresh yeast.

Yeast is composed of microor-
anisms (fungus cells, to be exact).
r its multiplication and growth,
ast requires air, moisture, heat
d nourishment (for example, in
e form of flour).

Yeast converts carbohydrates
our, sugar) into alcohol and
arbon dioxide, which is what
auses the dough to rise. The
eal temperature for raising
ough is 98° F. When filling the
read pan, make sure you add
e yeast last.

Sourdough: Sourdough is a
classic leavening agent for bread.
It's most important use is for
making breads and rolls with rye
flour lighter.

For beginners and weekend
bread bakers, it's easiest to buy
ready-made sourdough from
a store or mail order source.
Sourdough is available as a liquid
or dried. Most of the recipes in
this book call for dried sourdough.
If you prefer to use liquid sourdough, reduce the amount of
water by about the same weight
as the liquid sourdough. Be sure
to perform the touch test!

Milk and eggs: Milk also helps
bread rise. It makes the bread's
crumb more finely porous and
softer, and the bread stays fresh
longer and browns better. Non-fat
dry milk is best, because it has the
same dough enhancing properties
as milk but without the fat.

Eggs give bread color and flavor
and make the dough lighter. Both
whole eggs and yolks alone make
the dough easier to process and
keep the bread fresher longer.
1 egg equals ¼ cup water, so you
can substitute if desired.

Dough processed with milk
and/or egg spoils more easily
and can't be baked with the
timer function.

Flours and Meals

Wheat flour: Thanks to its high gluten content, wheat has the best baking properties. Our recipes use unbleached, all-purpose flour.

Spelt flour: Spelt is a member of the wheat family and also contains gluten, which is so important for baking. When unripe spelt is harvested and dried, it's sold as "green spelt."

Rye flour: Only sourdough can hydrolyze rye starch. Because of its low gluten content, rye is usually mixed with wheat flour.

Spelt

Wheat

Rye

Wheat

Six-grain

Four-grain

Quinoa

Corn

Amara

Whole-grain flours: The finer the flour is ground, the lighter the dough.

Whole-grain meal: Health food stores and well-stocked supermarkets offer both coarse whole meal and meal combinations (six-grain and four-grain). Dough made with coarse meal doesn't mix as well and tends to be heavy. When using, it is helpful to blend with unbleached, all-purpose flour.

Corn, kamut, quinoa and amaranth: Because most of these flours have very little gluten only small amounts (2–4 oz, or up to ¾ cup) should be substituted for wheat flour in these recipes.

Seeds, Sprouts, and Seasonings

Seeds: Sunflower seeds, pumpkin seeds, hemp seeds, buckwheat, soy nuts, psyllium seeds, etc., are favorite bread ingredients. They taste great and provide additional fiber. Toast them lightly to intensify their flavor.

Flaxseeds: Flaxseeds absorb water from the dough. If you add a lot of flaxseeds, you should soak them in an equal amount of water by weight to keep your baked goods from drying out. Remember to test the dough! Their moisture is subsequently transferred to the dough.

Sprouts: Regardless of type, sprouts are delicious in bread. Their flavors range from nutty, to mildly aromatic, to peppery and spicy. You can grow sprouts yourself, but they're also available in well-stocked supermarkets and health food stores.

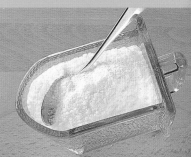

Bread seasonings: Bread seasonings include fennel, coriander, caraway, anise, cumin, pepper, herbes de Provence, thyme and marjoram. Seasonings are best when fresh or freshly ground, but you can also use dried.

Herbs: You can also add fresh garden herbs to your bread dough. But be careful not to alter the dough consistency too much. This could affect the final product.

Salt: When baking bread, never forget the salt. Salt adds flavor and also controls fermentation, meaning that salt makes a positive contribution to the shapeability and stability of the dough.

Baking Terminology

If you let the bread machine take care of the entire baking process, you won't have to do anything beyond measuring and loading ingredients. If you want to shape the dough yourself, however, you'll need to know certain technical baking terms that are used in these recipes.

Rising (Proofing)

As you become more adept at baking bread, it's important to be able to judge when the dough has fully risen. Otherwise, you won't be able to get the best results when you bake it in the oven. Press two fingers into the center of the dough. If the indentation stays, the dough has passed

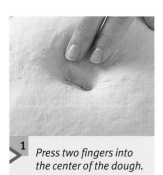

> **1** *Press two fingers into the center of the dough.*

the doubled-in-size stage and has risen too much. If, on the other hand, the dough is very resistant and the indentation closes up almost immediately, it's not ready yet.

For the best baked goods, you want the dough to be somewhere between these two states (not quite doubled in size). If you happen to forget your dough, all is not lost! Knead it thoroughly and let it rise again. After 30–40 minutes, bake it as usual.

If you don't re-knead over-risen dough, it will collapse in the oven.

Resting

After each kneading, the dough needs to rest so that the gluten can relax and the dough can regain its elasticity. Cover the dough with a cloth so it doesn't cool off or dry out. If you don't let the processed dough rest, its surface will crack and the dough won't take the proper shape.

Oven-rising

This is the first phase of the baking process. A temperature of about 120°F speeds up the yeast's production of fermentation gases, which expand even more in the heat. The ball of dough yields to this growing inner pressure and visibly grows by more than a third. To keep the surface from forming irregular cracks, brush or spray the dough with water, then score the surface with a sharp knife before placing it in the oven.

Rolling into a Cylinder

After rounding the dough (see facing page), let it rest for 5 minutes and then roll it into a cylinder shape.

Rounding

Rounding the dough makes it more porous, and therefore lighter and airier. At the same time, the ball of dough acquires a continuous, shiny skin. Only a rounded ball rises evenly and adopts the ideal shape. To round the dough, place it on a lightly floured surface. Touch the dough only briefly and quickly with your hands so it doesn't stick to you. This way, you can avoid adding too much flour, which would make the dough too dry. Always dust your hands with flour.

When you turn it around, the surface of the dough should be evenly stretched. This is important if you're going to bake the bread or rolls in the oven, because it ensures a uniform shape. By rounding the dough correctly, you also guarantee that any ingredients added later on in the process, such as nuts or seeds, will be worked evenly into the dough.

Fold

Place the dough on a floured work surface. Fold the far end of the dough over the near end.

Press Down

Dust your hands lightly with flour. With the heels of your hands, press down on the dough and push it away from yourself slightly.

Knead Thoroughly

Give the dough a quarter turn, then press down and push. Repeat several times until the dough is evenly and thoroughly kneaded.

Shape Loaf

Place the dough in a lightly floured dough rising basket with the seam side up, or place it on a baking sheet or in a greased pan with the seam side down.

Yeast Breads

The taste of yeast bread is beyond compare. Loaves are light and airy with a fine crumb, and have a thousand and one uses. Whether the added ingredients are sweet or a little spicy, yeast breads go with anything. It's best to enjoy them fresh!

Quick Recipes

Potato Bread

MAKES 1 LOAF

➤ 2 tsp salt | 2 tbs sugar | 3 tbs non-fat dry milk | 3 tbs softened butter | ¼ cup plus 1 tbs instant mashed potatoes | 20 oz (4¾ cups) unbleached all-purpose flour | 1½ tsp instant yeast

➤ Setting: White Bread
➤ Timer: Yes

1 | Place 1¾ cups water and remaining ingredients in the bread pan. Follow the operating instructions for your machine.

Variation: For **Bacon Bread**, add ½ cup diced smoked bacon, 1 tsp bread seasonings, ½ cup sunflower seeds and 2 tablespoons water to the basic dough.

Butter Bread

MAKES 1 LOAF

➤ 2 tsp salt | 16 oz (3¾ cups) unbleached all-purpose flour | 1 tsp sugar | 4 tbs softened butter | 1½ tsp instant yeast

➤ Setting: Standard or White Bread
➤ Timer: Yes

1 | Place 1⅓ cups water and remaining ingredients in the pan. Follow the operating instructions for your machine.

Variation: Bake bread in a greased loaf pan. To do so, remove the dough from the machine, knead it and roll it into a cylinder 10 inches long. Divide into equal thirds and place side-by-side in the loaf pan. Preheat oven to 350°F. Let dough rest for 40 minutes, then brush with water. Bake for 25–30 minutes (bottom rack).

13

Easy

Herb Butter Bread

MAKES 1 LOAF

➤ 1 tsp salt
  4 tbs softened butter
  ½ cup cream cheese
  2 tbs chopped fresh herbs
  16 oz (3¾ cups) unbleached all-purpose flour
  2 tsp instant yeast

🕐 Prep time: 15 minutes
  Setting: Standard
🕐 Timer: Yes
➤ Calories per slice (10 slices): About 220

1 | Place 1⅓ cups water and remaining ingredients in the bread pan in the specified order. Follow the operating instructions for your machine.

➤ Great with ham or smoked salmon.

➤ Variation:

  Party Rolls

  Use this dough to make mini party rolls. Shape them so they're half the size of standard rolls.

For Picnics

Sprout Bread

MAKES 1 LOAF

➤ 2 tsp salt
  3 tbs olive oil
  2 tbs vinegar
  Freshly ground pepper
  16 oz (3¾ cups) unbleached all-purpose flour
  1½ tsp instant yeast
  ¾ cup mixed sprouts

🕐 Prep time: 15 minutes
  Setting: White Bread or Standard
🕐 Timer: Yes
➤ Calories per slice (10 slices): About 190

1 | Place 1½ cups water and all remaining ingredients except sprouts in the bread pan in the specified order. Followthe operating instructions for your machine.

2 | After 30 minutes or after the beep, add the sprouts to the bread pan.

TIP

Grow your own sprouts

It's easy to grow your favorite sprouts at home. From your local health food store, you can purchase germinable seeds and seed combinations. Soak small to medium-sized seeds for 4–6 hours and large seeds for 12–15 hours. Place the seeds in a sprout jar or container (special sprouters are ideal). Fill the jar no more than one-quarter full so the seeds have sufficient light and air. Rinse the sprouts twice a day with fresh water. After one day, the first sprouts will start to emerge. The sprouts are ready when they reach a certain length. For example, alfalfa sprouts reach their peak in 4–6 days, cress in 7 days, radish sprouts in 3–4 days, etc.

Hearty and Nutty

Buckwheat Sunflower Bread

MAKES 1 LOAF

- ➤ ½ cup buckwheat
- ¼ cup sunflower seeds
- 1½ tsp salt
- 2 tbs honey
- 16 oz (3¾ cups) unbleached all-purpose flour
- 1½ tsp instant yeast

⏱ Prep time: 15 minutes
  Setting: Standard
⏱ Timer: Yes
➤ Calories per slice (10 slices): About 210

1 | Toast buckwheat in an ungreased pan until golden brown. Let cool and crack on a cutting board with a rolling pin or in a food processor. Toast sunflower seeds if desired in order to intensify their flavor.

2 | Place 1⅓ cups water and remaining ingredients in the bread pan in the following order: Salt, honey, sunflower seeds, buckwheat, flour and yeast. Follow the operating instructions for your machine.

Easy

Spelt Cottage Cheese Bread

MAKES 1 LOAF

- ➤ 1 tsp salt
- 1 cup cottage cheese
- 3 tbs sunflower oil
- 7 oz (1½ cups) whole spelt flour
- 10 oz (2⅓ cups) unbleached all-purpose flour
- 1½ tsp instant yeast

⏱ Prep time: 15 minutes
  Setting: Standard
⏱ Timer: Yes
➤ Calories per slice (10 slices): About 220

TIP Although the whole-grain flour reduces rising, it also makes the bread moist and very delicious. This bread is excellent with a cheese plate, or with smoked salmon.

1 | Place 1 cup water and all remaining ingredients in the bread pan in the specified order. Follow the operating instructions for your machine.

➤ Variation:

Bread Waffles

Prepare the dough (setting: Dough cycle). If desired, you can add 3 teaspoons bread seasonings or sesame seeds. After the beep, remove the dough from the machine and cook it in a waffle iron in batches. These crispy waffles will keep for several days in a sealed tin.

Photo bottom: Spelt Cottage Cheese Bread   *Photo top:* Buckwheat Sunflower Bread ➤

For Company | Spicy
Hunter's Bread

MAKES 1 LOAF

- ➤ **2 tsp salt**

    3 tbs chopped roasted
    red peppers

    2 tsp crushed red
    chile pepper

    ¼ cup sunflower seeds

    3 tbs fresh cream or
    crème fraîche

    17 oz (4 cups) unbleached
    all-purpose flour

    1 tsp instant yeast

- ⏲ Prep time: 15 minutes

    Setting: Standard
- ⏲ Timer: Yes
- ➤ Calories per slice (10
    slices): About 200

1 | Place 1⅓ cups water and
all remaining ingredients
in the bread pan in the
specified order. Follow the
operating instructions for
your machine.

- ➤ Excellent with soup or pâté.

Transportable
Sandwich Bread

MAKES 1 LOAF

- ➤ **1 tsp salt**

    3 tbs mustard (sweet
    or hot)

    1 tsp green peppercorns

    16 oz (3¾ cups) unbleached
    all-purpose flour

    1½ tsp instant yeast

    1 tbs caraway seeds
    (optional)

- ⏲ Prep time: 15 minutes

    Setting: White Bread
    or Standard
- ⏲ Timer: Yes
- ➤ Calories per slice (10
    slices): About 160

1 | Place 1½ cups water and
all remaining ingredients
in the bread pan in the
specified order. Follow the
operating instructions for
your machine.

- ➤ **Classic Club Sandwich**

Slice bread, toast and let
cool. Spread 1 slice with
mayonnaise and top with
deli-sliced chicken or
turkey breast and lettuce
leaves. Spread the next
slice with mayonnaise and
place on top of lettuce. Top
with bacon and tomato and
another piece of toast. Cut
sandwich in half diagonally
and serve.

- ➤ Variation:

Sausage Crescent Rolls

To make 16 crescent rolls,
shape dough into 2 balls
and let rest for 5 minutes.
Line a baking sheet with
parchment paper. Preheat
oven to 400°F. Roll out
dough into 2 circles (each
with a 10 inch diameter).
Cut each circle into eighths
and roll out these triangles
to make them slightly larger.
Place 1 Vienna sausage
at the long end of each
triangle and roll up tightly
from the wide end into
a crescent. Place on the
baking sheet and let rest
for 20 minutes. Brush with
egg yolk and bake in the
oven (middle rack) for
20–25 minutes until
golden-brown.

For a Buffet

Cottage Cheese and Corn Bread

MAKES 1 LOAF

➤ ½ seeded and diced red bell pepper (about 2 oz)

½ cup cottage cheese

½ cup canned or thawed frozen corn

1 tbs capers

2 tsp salt

16 oz (3¾ cups) unbleached all-purpose flour

1½ tsp instant yeast

🕐 Prep time: 20 minutes
Setting: Standard

🕐 Timer: Yes

➤ Calories per slice (10 slices): About 170

1 | Clean bell pepper, rinse and dice finely. Place 1 cup water and remaining ingredients in the bread pan in the following order: Cottage cheese, corn, bell pepper, capers, salt, flour and yeast. Follow the operating instructions for your machine.

➤ Using leftovers: Use leftover ingredients to make a salad. Clean the rest of the bell pepper, rinse and dice finely. Peel 1 small onion and dice finely. Combine bell pepper, onion, ½ cup cottage cheese and ½ cup corn. Season with 2 tablespoons vinegar, pepper and salt and let marinate for at least 30 minutes.

Mediterranean

Feta Olive Bread

MAKES 1 LOAF

➤ ½ cup sliced, pitted black olives

½ cup crumbled feta cheese

2 tbs olive oil

1 tbs herbes de Provence

1 tsp salt

16 oz (3¾ cups) unbleached all-purpose flour

1½ tsp instant yeast

🕐 Prep time: 20 minutes
Setting: White Bread

🕐 Timer: Yes

➤ Calories per slice (10 slices): About 190

1 | Place 1 cup water and remaining ingredients in the bread pan in the following order: Olive oil, herbs, feta, olives, salt, flour and yeast. Follow the operating instructions for your machine.

➤ Delicious with a Greek salad and a glass of retsina.

➤ Variation:
Flatbread

Prepare dough (setting: Dough cycle). After the beep, remove the dough from the machine. Round the dough and let rest briefly. Line a baking sheet with parchment paper. Shape dough into one 12 inch diameter flatbread and place on the baking sheet. Preheat oven to 425°F. Let dough rest for 30 minutes. Shortly before baking, pierce dough several times with a fork. Bake in the oven (middle rack) for 15–20 minutes until golden. Remove, brush with olive oil or garlic butter and sprinkle with herbes de Provence.

Photo bottom: **Cottage Cheese and Corn Bread**   *Photo top:* **Feta Olive Bread** ➤

For Company
Smoked Salmon Bread

MAKES 1 LOAF

➤ **3 tbs dill**
½ cup sliced smoked salmon (4 oz)
1 tsp salt
1 tbs mustard
2 tbs horseradish (optional)
3 tbs capers (optional)
18 oz (4¼ cups) unbleached all-purpose flour
1½ tsp instant yeast

🕐 Prep time: 20 minutes
  Setting: Standard or Quick
🕐 Timer: Yes
➤ Calories per slice (10 slices): About 210

1 │ Rinse dill, pat dry, strip off leaves and chop finely

2 │ Chop smoked salmon into small dice and mix with 1 tablespoon flour to keep pieces from sticking together.

3 │ Place 1⅓ cups water and all remaining ingredients in the bread pan in the specified order. Follow the operating instructions for your machine.

➤ Serve with hard-boiled eggs, cream cheese and sparkling wine.

For a Picnic
Italian Tomato Bread

MAKES 1 LOAF

➤ **2 tsp salt**
1 tsp chopped fresh thyme or basil
1 tsp pesto (homemade or from a jar)
3 oz shredded mozzarella cheese
18 oz (4¼ cups) unbleached all-purpose flour
2 tsp instant yeast
3 tsp crushed chile peppers (optional)
1 cup peeled, seeded and diced tomatoes

🕐 Prep time: 25 minutes
  Setting: Standard
🕐 Timer: Yes
➤ Calories per slice (10 slices): About 190

1 │ Place ½ cup water and all remaining ingredients in the bread pan in the following order: Salt, herbs, pesto, mozzarella, flour, yeast, chile peppers and tomatoes.

2 │ After 20 minutes, test the dough. Add a little water or flour as needed.

➤ Topping: Drizzle bread slices with olive oil and top with basil and mozzarella.

Easy
Seeded Cream Bread

MAKES 1 LOAF

- ➤ 2 tsp salt
  - $\frac{1}{2}$ tbs dried thyme
  - $\frac{1}{4}$ cup sunflower seeds
  - $\frac{1}{4}$ cup pumpkin seeds
  - $\frac{1}{2}$ cup fresh cream or crème fraîche
  - 16 oz ($3\frac{3}{4}$ cups) unbleached all-purpose flour
  - 2 tsp instant yeast

- ◷ Prep time: 15 minutes
  - Setting: Standard
- ◷ Timer: Yes
- ➤ Calories per slice (10 slices): About 220

1 | Place 1 cup water and all remaining ingredients in the bread pan in the specified order. Follow the operating instructions for your machine.

- ➤ This bread is ideal for sandwiches.

TIP If you want the seeds to remain whole, add them after the beep or after about 30 minutes.

Hearty
Pumpkin Bread

MAKES 1 LOAF

- ➤ 1 tbs freshly grated ginger root
  - $1\frac{1}{2}$ cups canned or fresh pumpkin puree (16 oz ; not pie filling)
  - 1 egg
  - 2 tsp salt
  - 1 tsp sugar
  - $\frac{1}{2}$ tsp freshly ground pepper
  - 1 pinch nutmeg
  - $\frac{1}{4}$ cup pumpkin seeds
  - 13 oz (3 cups) unbleached all-purpose flour
  - 3.5 oz ($\frac{2}{3}$ cup) cornmeal
  - $1\frac{1}{2}$ tsp instant yeast

- ◷ Prep time: 30 minutes
  - Setting: Standard
- ◷ Timer: No
- ➤ Calories per slice (10 slices): About 270

1 | Place $\frac{1}{3}$ cup plus 1 tablespoon water and all remaining ingredients in the bread pan. Follow operating instructions for your machine.

For Company
Halloween Pumpkin Bread

MAKES 1 LOAF

- ➤ $\frac{3}{4}$ cup canned or fresh pumpkin puree (8 oz; not pie filling)
  - 2 tsp salt
  - 4 tbs brown sugar
  - $1\frac{1}{2}$ tsp cinnamon
  - 1 pinch ground cloves
  - 1 tsp freshly grated ginger root
  - $1\frac{1}{2}$ tbs softened butter
  - 15 oz ($3\frac{1}{2}$ cups) unbleached all-purpose flour
  - $1\frac{1}{2}$ tsp instant yeast
  - $\frac{1}{3}$ cup raisins

- ◷ Prep time: 20 minutes
  - Setting: Standard
- ◷ Timer: Yes
- ➤ Calories per slice (10 slices): About 200

1 | Place $\frac{3}{4}$ cup water and all remaining ingredients except for the raisins in the bread pan. Add raisins to the pan 30 minutes after starting the cycle. Follow the operating instructions for your machine.

Sweet | Easy
Raisin Bread

MAKES 1 LOAF
- 2 tsp salt

  4 tbs sugar

  3 tbs softened butter

  16 oz (3¾ cups) unbleached all-purpose flour

  1½ tsp instant yeast

  1½ tsp ground cinnamon (optional)

  3 tbs non-fat dry milk (optional)

  ½ cup raisins

- Prep time: 15 minutes

  Setting: White Bread
- Timer: Yes
- Calories per slice (10 slices): About 240

1 | Place 1½ cups water and all remaining ingredients except for raisins in the bread pan in the specified order. Follow the operating instructions for your machine.

2 | Add raisins to the pan 30 minutes after starting the cycle or after the beep.

- A real treat when toasted and buttered.

Middle-Eastern | Sweet

Date Bread with Raisins

MAKES 1 LOAF
- ½ cup dates

  1 tsp salt

  1 egg

  2 tbs cocoa powder

  1 pinch ground cloves

  1 pinch ground cinnamon

  6 tbs sugar

  ½ cup sesame seeds

  ½ cup slivered almonds

  ¼ cup raisins

  16 oz (3¾ cups) unbleached all-purpose flour

  1½ tsp instant yeast

- Prep time: 20 minutes

  Setting: Standard
- Timer: No
- Calories per slice (10 slices): About 300

1 | Pit dates, cut into quarters and place in the bread pan. Place 1¼ cups water and all remaining ingredients in the bread pan in the specified order. Follow the operating instructions for your machine.

- Variation:

  Middle-Eastern Cake

  Prepare dough (setting: Dough cycle). Remove the dough from the machine and transfer to a greased 10 inch springform pan. Let rest for 30 minutes. Brush with water and top with 13 walnut halves (12 around the edges and 1 in the center) and 12 peeled almonds. Bake in an oven preheated to 325°F (middle rack) for 30-35 minutes. While still warm, brush with honey. A specialty from the Thousand and One Nights!

Easy
Muesli Bread

MAKES 1 LOAF

➤ **1 tsp salt**
2 tbs sunflower oil
14 oz (4½ cups) unbleached all-purpose flour
1½ cups muesli
1½ tsp instant yeast

🕐 Prep time: 15 minutes
Setting: Standard or Quick
🕐 Timer: Yes
➤ Calories per slice (10 slices): About 210

1 │ Place 1½ cups water and all remaining ingredients in the bread pan in the specified order. Follow the operating instructions for your machine.

➤ Variations:
Muesli Bran Bread
To fortify the bread with even more healthy fiber, replace 3 ounces (⅔ cup) of the flour with wheat or oat bran.

Muesli Rolls
You can also turn the dough into 12 Muesli Rolls (setting: Dough cycle). Use the quick recipe for rolls on page 47.

For Sunday Breakfast
Apricot Bread

MAKES 1 LOAF

➤ **1 tsp salt**
4 tbs apricot jam
½ cup sliced almonds
3 tbs orange liqueur (optional)
2 tbs softened butter
16 oz (3¾ cups) unbleached all-purpose flour
1½ tsp instant yeast

🕐 Prep time: 15 minutes
Setting: Standard or Quick
🕐 Timer: Yes
➤ Calories per slice (10 slices): About 240

TIP
To make the bread even fruitier, add 3 tablespoons candied orange peel.

1 │ Place 1⅓ cups water and all remaining ingredients in the bread pan in the specified order. Follow the operating instructions for your machine.

➤ Variations:
Instead of apricot jam, use orange marmalade. This bread is also delicious with sour cherry jam and cherry brandy combined with 3 tablespoons chocolate sprinkles.

To make a more nutritious bread, replace 4½ ounces (1 cup) of the flour with whole spelt flour.

➤ **Suitable Spreads:**
Honey cream cheese: combine 1 cup cream cheese, 6 tablespoons aromatic honey (for example, chestnut or heather honey) and 1 pinch saffron.

Prune or apricot cream cheese: purée ¾ cup pitted prunes or apricots and stir in 1 cup cream cheese, 6 tablespoons lemon juice and 1 pinch ground cinnamon.

Exotic

Yogurt Banana Bread

MAKES 1 LOAF

- ➤ ¾ cup mashed banana
  1 tsp salt
  4 tbs butter
  ¼ cup honey
  ½ tsp ground cinnamon
  2 oz (½ cup) ground almonds or almond flour
  1 cup yogurt
  16 oz (3¾ cups) unbleached all-purpose flour
  1½ tsp instant yeast

- 🕐 Prep time: 20 minutes
  Setting: Standard
- 🕐 Timer: No
- ➤ Calories per slice (10 slices): About 270

1 │ Place ¼ cup water in the bread pan. Add all remaining ingredients to the bread pan. Follow the operating instructions for your machine.

- ➤ Variation:
  Instead of bananas, use 1 cup applesauce and ¾ cup yogurt.

Easy

Brioche

MAKES 1 LOAF

- ➤ 1½ tsp salt
  ¼ cup sugar
  1 egg
  2 egg yolks
  ¾ cup (1½ sticks) softened butter
  18 oz (4¼ cups) unbleached all-purpose flour
  3 tbs non-fat dry milk
  1 tsp instant yeast

- 🕐 Prep time: 15 minutes
  Setting: Standard
- 🕐 Timer: No
- ➤ Calories per slice (12 slices): About 280

1 │ Place ⅔ cup water and all remaining ingredients in the bread pan in the specified order. Follow the operating instructions for your machine.

- ➤ Variation:
  Chocolate Brioche
  Setting: Standard
  After 30 minutes, add ¾ cup chocolate chips.

- ➤ Using leftovers:
  French Toast
  Cut leftover brioche (which may also be a little dry) into 1 inch thick slices. For 4 slices, whisk together 1 egg and ¾ cup milk and briefly soak slices in this mixture. In a nonstick pan, heat 2–3 tablespoons butter per slice. Fry each brioche slice in butter for 3–4 minutes on each side until crispy and golden-brown. Immediately transfer to a plate, sprinkle with cinnamon sugar and serve warm with maple syrup.

Photo bottom: **Brioche**   *Photo top:* **Yogurt Banana Bread** ➤

Sourdough Breads

Firm and hearty, who can resist the fragrance of a loaf of freshly baked country or farm bread? Try our multigrain sourdough breads and delicious French bread with fresh butter and you're likely to become addicted.

Dry sourdough starter is available from mail order and online sources (www.bakerscatalogue.com). Our recipes include measurements for Lalvain dry sourdough starter. If using another brand, please follow manufacturer suggestions for one loaf of bread.

Quick Recipes

Multigrain Rye Bread

MAKES 1 LOAF

➤ 2 tsp salt
  ½ tbs rye malt (optional)
  ½ tsp ground caraway seeds
  2 tbs vinegar
  ⅛ tsp dry sourdough starter
  9 oz (2 cups) rye flour
  7 oz (1⅔ cups) unbleached
  all-purpose flour
  1½ tsp instant yeast

➤ Setting: White Bread or Standard
➤ Timer: Yes

1 | Place 1⅓ cups water and all remaining ingredients in the bread pan in the specified order. Follow the operating instructions for your machine.

Multigrain Wheat Bread

MAKES 1 LOAF

➤ 2 tsp salt
  ⅛ tsp dry sourdough starter
  8.5 oz (2 cups) unbleached
  all-purpose flour
  5 oz (1 cup) whole wheat flour
  5 oz (1 cup) rye flour
  1½ tsp instant yeast

➤ Setting: Standard
➤ Timer: Yes

1 | Place 1½ cups water and all remaining ingredients in the bread pan in the specified order. Follow the operating instructions for your machine.

Nutty

Sunflower Bread

MAKES 1 LOAF

- ➤ 3 tsp salt
  $\frac{1}{8}$ tsp dry sourdough starter
  3.5 oz ($\frac{3}{4}$ cup) rye flour
  13 oz (3 cups) unbleached all-purpose flour
  $\frac{3}{4}$ cups sunflower seeds
  1 tsp dry yeast

- Prep time: 15 minutes
  Setting: Standard
- Timer: Yes
- ➤ Calories per slice (15 slices): About 170

1 | Place 1$\frac{1}{2}$ cups water and all remaining ingredients except the sunflower seeds in the bread pan in the specified order. Add the sunflower seeds after about 30 minutes. Follow the operating instructions for your machine.

- ➤ Variation:

  Soy Bread

  Instead of sunflower seeds, use roasted soy nuts.

Hearty

Rustic Country Bread

MAKES 1 LOAF

- ➤ 2 tsp salt
  1 tbs bread seasonings
  $\frac{1}{2}$ tbs rye malt
  $\frac{1}{8}$ tsp dry sourdough starter
  5 oz (1 cup) whole rye flour
  13 oz (3 cups) unbleached all-purpose flour
  1 tsp instant yeast

- Prep time: 15 minutes
  Setting: Standard
- Timer: Yes
- ➤ Calories per slice (15 slices): About 120

1 | Place 1$\frac{1}{2}$ cups water and all remaining ingredients in the bread pan in the specified order. Follow the operating instructions for your machine.

- ➤ Great with dry-cured meats and cheeses.

Easy
Caraway Bread

MAKES 1 LOAF

➤ 2 tsp salt

2 tbs caraway seeds

⅛ tsp dry
sourdough starter

2.5 oz (½ cup) rye flour

14 oz (3½ cups) unbleached
all-purpose flour

1½ tsp dry yeast

🕐 Prep time: 15 minutes
Setting: White Bread

🕐 Timer: Yes

➤ Calories per slice (10
slices): About 170

1 | Place 1½ cups water and
all remaining ingredients in
the bread pan in the specified
order. Follow the operating
instructions for your machine.

➤ Goes with cold pork roast,
coleslaw and beer.

Classic
French Bread

MAKES 1 LOAF

➤ 2 tsp salt

½ tbs rye malt

19 oz (4½ cups) unbleached
all-purpose flour

⅛ tsp dry
sourdough starter

1½ tsp instant yeast

🕐 Prep time: 15 minutes
Setting: White Bread
or French

🕐 Timer: Yes

➤ Calories per slice (10
slices): About 180

1 | Place 1¾ cups water and
all remaining ingredients in
the bread pan in the specified
order. Follow the operating
instructions for your machine.

➤ Variations:

Baguettes
Prepare the dough (setting:
Dough cycle). Remove
finished dough from the
machine, knead briefly and
divide in half. Do not round
the dough or the pores of
the crumb will be too fine.

Roll the two halves into
cylinders and place side-
by-side on a baking sheet
lined with parchment
paper. Cover with a damp
cloth and let rest in a warm
place for 40 minutes.
Preheat oven to 500°F.
Then cut about five long,
deep slits along the tops
with a sharp knife. Spray
with water. Bake for 10
minutes (middle rack), then
reduce heat to 400°F and
bake for 15-20 minutes
until done.

Classic French Bread

You can also prepare this
bread without sourdough.
In this case, combine 1¾
cups water, 2 teaspoons
salt, 20 ounces (4¾ cups)
unbleached all-purpose
flour and 1½ teaspoons
instant yeast in the
bread pan.

Like the recipe above, you
can prepare this dough
using the Dough cycle
setting and shape by hand
into baguettes.

Photo bottom: **Baguettes (variation)**   *Photo top:* **Caraway Bread** ➤

Hearty | Spicy
Farm Bread

MAKES 1 LOAF

➤ 2 tsp salt

1 tsp each of ground caraway seeds and ground coriander seeds

1 cup liquid sourdough starter

½ tbs rye malt

7 oz (1⅓ cups) rye flour

14 oz (3⅓ cups) unbleached all-purpose flour

1½ tsp instant yeast

🕐 Prep time: 15 minutes
Setting: Standard
🕐 Timer: Yes
➤ Calories per slice (10 slices): About 220

1 | Place 1½ cups water and all remaining ingredients in the bread pan in the specified order. Follow the operating instructions for your machine.

For a Buffet
Herb Bread

MAKES 1 LOAF

➤ 1 clove garlic, chopped

1 tbs each chopped fresh parsley, chopped chives, thyme, oregano and rosemary (substitute ½ tsp each dried)

1½ tsp salt

Freshly ground pepper

4 tbs butter

⅛ tsp dry sourdough starter

16 oz (3¾ cups) unbleached all-purpose flour

1 tsp instant yeast

🕐 Prep time: 15 minutes
Setting: Standard
🕐 Timer: Yes
➤ Calories per slice (10 slices): About 200

1 | Place 1½ cups water and all remaining ingredients in the bread pan in the specified order. Follow the operating instructions for your machine.

➤ **Salmon Cream Cheese**

Combine 1 cup cream cheese with 3 tablespoons sour cream. Finely dice 1 cup smoked salmon. Rinse 1 small bunch dill, strip off leaves and chop finely. Stir salmon and dill into the cheese and season to taste with pepper.

TIP You can also replace a fresh herb with ½ teaspoon of a dried herb.

Hearty

Meal and Seed Bread

MAKES 1 LOAF

➤ 1 tsp salt

3 tbs vinegar

1/2 cup mixed seeds (sunflower seeds, pumpkin seeds, flaxseeds, sesame seeds, etc.)

1/8 tsp dry sourdough starter

7 oz (1 1/3 cup) fine spelt meal

8.5 oz (2 cups) unbleached all-purpose flour

1 1/2 tsp instant yeast

1 1/2 tsp bread seasonings (optional)

🕐 Prep time: 15 minutes

Setting: Standard

🕐 Timer: Yes

➤ Calories per slice (13 slices): About 160

1 | Place 1 1/4 cups water and all remaining ingredients in the bread pan in the specified order. Follow the operating instructions for your machine.

Snacktime Classic

Country Bread

MAKES 1 LOAF

➤ 2 tsp salt

1/2 tbs rye malt

1/2 tsp ground or 2 tsp whole caraway seeds

3.5 oz (3/4 cup) rye flour

1/8 tsp dry sourdough starter

12 oz (2 3/4 cups) unbleached all-purpose flour

2 tsp instant yeast

🕐 Prep time: 15 minutes

Setting: White Bread or longer cycle

🕐 Timer: Yes

➤ Calories per slice (10 slices): About 160

1 | Place 1 1/3 cups water and all remaining ingredients in the bread pan in the specified order. Follow the operating instructions for your machine.

➤ Variation:

Sausages Wrapped in Dough

For 6 servings, you need 2 pounds cooked pork sausages. Prepare the Country Bread dough (setting: Dough cycle), also adding 5 tablespoons sesame seeds.

Remove the dough from the machine and roll it out. Pat sausages dry and wrap them up in the dough. Line a baking sheet with parchment paper. Place dough-wrapped sausages on the baking sheet with the seam side down. Preheat oven to 400°F. Let dough rest for 30 minutes, then brush with water and bake in the oven (bottom rack) for 1 1/2 hours.

Great with a green salad.

Photo left: **Country Bread** *Photo right:* **Meal and Seed Bread** ➤

Easy

Pumpkin Seed Bread

MAKES 1 LOAF

➤ 2 tsp salt

⅛ tsp dry sourdough starter

3 tbs sunflower oil

½ cup pumpkin seeds

3.5 oz (⅔ cup) whole spelt flour

13 oz (3 cups) unbleached all-purpose flour

2 tsp instant yeast

🕐 Prep time: 15 minutes

Setting: Standard or Whole Grain

🕐 Timer: Yes

➤ Calories per slice (10 slices): About 240

1 | Place 1⅓ cups water and all remaining ingredients in the bread pan in the specified order. Follow the operating instructions for your machine.

➤ Variation:

Instead of pumpkin seeds, use sunflower seeds or sunflower sprouts.

Takes More Time

Whole Grain Bread

MAKES 1 LOAF

➤ For the pre-dough:

5 oz (1 cup) spelt meal

➤ For the dough:

7 oz (1⅓ cups) whole spelt flour

10.5 oz (2 cups) whole wheat flour

3 tbs vinegar

2 tsp salt

1½ tsp instant yeast

🕐 Prep time: 3 days

Setting: Standard or Whole Grain

🕐 Timer: No

➤ Calories per slice (10 slices): About 210

1 | For the pre-dough, combine spelt meal and ½ cup lukewarm water and let stand overnight at room temperature.

2 | The next morning, stir 3.5 ounces (⅔ cup) whole spelt flour and ⅓ cup water into the pre-dough. Let stand overnight at room temperature.

3 | On the third morning, place ¾ cup water and all remaining ingredients in the bread pan in the specified order. Follow the operating instructions for your machine.

➤ Variation:

Whole Spelt Bread

To make this simple yet very good bread, place 1⅔ cups water in the bread pan. Add 2 teaspoons salt, 14 ounces (2⅔ cups) whole spelt flour, 4.25 ounces (1 cup) unbleached all-purpose flour, 2 teaspoons bread seasonings (optional) and 2 teaspoons yeast. Prepare using the Whole Grain cycle.

For Company
Onion Bread

MAKES 1 LOAF

- ¼ cup diced bacon
  1 tbs minced rosemary
  1 onion, minced
  1½ tsp salt
  ⅛ tsp dry sourdough starter
  16 oz (3¾ cups) unbleached all-purpose flour
  3.5 oz (¾ cup) rye flour
  1½ tsp instant yeast

- ⏱ Prep time: 20 minutes
  Setting: White Bread or Standard
- ⏱ Timer: Yes
- ➤ Calories per slice (10 slices): About 190

1 | Fry bacon in a pan until translucent. Add rosemary and cook for 1 minute. Add onion and cook until translucent, about 4 minutes. Allow to cool completely.

2 | Place 1⅓ cups water and then all remaining ingredients in the bread pan. Follow the operating instructions for your machine.

- ➤ Delicious alone or dipped into cheese fondue.

➤ Variation:

Onion Flatbread

Roll out dough into a flatbread with a 12 inch diameter and pierce several times with a fork. Preheat oven to 425°F. Bake flatbread for 15–20 minutes (middle rack).

For a Buffet
Walnut Bread

MAKES 1 LOAF

- ➤ ½ cup chopped walnuts
  1 tsp salt
  3 tbs walnut oil
  11 oz (2½ cups) unbleached all-purpose flour
  3.5 oz (¾ cup) rye flour
  ⅛ tsp dry sourdough starter
  1 tsp instant yeast

- ⏱ Prep time: 20 minutes
  Setting: White Bread
- ⏱ Timer: No
- ➤ Calories per slice (10 slices): About 220

1 | Place 1⅓ cups water and all remaining ingredients except the walnuts in the bread pan in the specified order. Follow the operating instructions for your machine.

2 | After 30 minutes or after the beep, add chopped walnuts.

- ➤ Variations:

Assorted Nuts

Instead of walnuts, you can also use almonds, peanuts, hazelnuts, pecans or macadamia nuts. If you can't find unsalted macadamia nuts, use the roasted and salted kind and leave the salt out of the dough.

Crispy Nut Bars

Prepare the dough using the Dough cycle. Spread 2 cups coarsely chopped, mixed nuts, ½ cup sesame seeds and a little coarse salt on a work surface. Roll out bread dough onto the nut-salt mixture and cut it into strips using a pizza cutter or suitable knife. Preheat oven to 400°F. Place strips on a baking sheet lined with parchment paper and let rest for 30 minutes. Spray with water and sprinkle with salt. Bake in the oven (middle rack) for 20 minutes until crispy.

Shaped Breads

Your bread machine can also serve as an alternative to a traditional bread-kneading machine. It saves time and lets you prepare perfect dough under ideal conditions. Bake your own Sunday rolls for a change, and you'll be amazed to find out that they're the best you've had in a long time. Guaranteed!

Quick Recipes

Rolls

MAKES 12 ROLLS

➤ 1 tsp salt | 1 tsp sugar | 19 oz (4¼ cups) unbleached all-purpose flour | 1½ tsp instant yeast

➤ Setting: Dough cycle

1 | Place 1⅔ cups water and all remaining ingredients in the bread pan.

2 | Briefly knead the dough. Line a baking sheet with parchment paper. Divide dough into 12 pieces, round each piece and place on the baking sheet. Let rest for 5 minutes, then cover with a damp cloth and let rest for another 30 minutes. Preheat the oven to 400°F.

3 | Moisten the dough balls and score with scissors. Bake for 20–25 minutes (middle rack).

Country Wheat Bread

MAKES 1 LOAF

➤ 2 tsp salt | 8.5 oz (2 cups) unbleached all-purpose flour | 7 oz (1⅓ cup) whole wheat flour | 3.5 oz (¾ cup) rye flour | ½ cup cottage cheese | ⅛ tsp dry sourdough starter | 1 tsp instant yeast

➤ Setting: Dough cycle

1 | Place 1⅓ cups water and all remaining ingredients in the bread pan. Round the dough, place it in a floured dough rising basket, press down and sprinkle with flour. Cover and let rest for 30 minutes. Preheat oven to 500°F. Line a baking sheet with parchment paper.

2 | Reverse the dough onto the baking sheet. Brush with water and score. Bake for 15 minutes (middle rack) at 500°F and then 35–40 minutes at 325°F.

47

Classic | For Company

Bagels

MAKES 9 BAGELS

➤ 1½ tsp salt
  1 tsp sugar
  18 oz (4½ cups) unbleached all-purpose flour
  2 tsp dry yeast

🕐 Prep time: 30 minutes
🕐 Resting time: 35 minutes
🕐 Baking time: 25 minutes
  Setting: Dough cycle
➤ Calories per bagel: About 190

1 | Place 1⅓ cups water and all remaining ingredients in the bread pan in the specified order. Follow the operating instructions for your machine.

2 | Remove the dough from the machine, divide into 9 pieces (3 ounces each) and round. Let rest for 5 minutes. Flatten balls slightly, make a depression in the center with your finger and sprinkle in a little flour. Poke your finger all the way through and turn the dough on your finger while widening the hole to about 1½ inches. Let rest on a lightly floured surface for 30 minutes.

3 | Line a baking sheet with parchment paper and preheat the oven to 400°F. In the meantime, fill a wide pot with water and bring to a boil. Lower dough rings into the lightly simmering water with the top sides down. After 30 seconds, turn. Remove bagels from the water and drain on a kitchen towel. The towel will soak up the excess water.

4 | Place bagels on the baking sheet and bake in the oven (middle rack) for 20–25 minutes until golden-brown. Transfer to a rack to cool.

➤ Serve with cream cheese and smoked salmon

1 Round
Round each piece of dough with floured hands (also see page 11).

2 Make a hole
It's easy to make and shape the hole with your finger.

3 Boil
Before baking, briefly simmer bagels in boiling water.

49

Hearty

Multigrain Rolls

MAKES 10 ROLLS

➤ 1½ tsp salt

½ tbs rye malt

⅛ tsp dry sourdough starter

5 oz (1 cup) rye flour

9 oz (1¾ cups) spelt flour

3 oz (⅔ cup) whole wheat flour

3 tbs non-fat dry milk

1 tsp instant yeast

➤ Plus:

Flour for the work surface

🕐 Prep time: 30 minutes

🕐 Resting time: 35 minutes

🕐 Baking time: 25 minutes
Setting: Dough cycle

🕐 Timer: Yes

➤ Calories per roll: About 200

1 | Place 2 cups water and all remaining ingredients in the bread pan. Follow the operating instructions for your machine.

2 | Remove the dough from the machine and knead briefly. Divide dough into 10 balls, round and roll into cylinders. Line a baking sheet with parchment paper. Place rolls on the baking sheet and let rest for 5 minutes, then press a little flatter. Cover with a cloth and let rest for 30 minutes. Preheat oven to 400°F.

3 | Before baking, brush with water and score with a knife. Bake for 20–25 minutes (middle rack).

For Company

Breakfast Crescent Rolls

MAKES 16 CRESCENT ROLLS

➤ 1 tsp salt

1 tbs sugar

½ cup (1 stick) softened butter

1 egg

20 oz (4¾ cups) unbleached all-purpose flour

3 tbs non-fat dry milk (optional)

1 tsp instant yeast

➤ Plus:

Flour for the work surface

1 egg yolk for brushing on surface

🕐 Prep time: 25 minutes

🕐 Resting time: 35 minutes

🕐 Baking time: 25 minutes
Setting: Dough cycle

🕐 Timer: No

➤ Calories per roll: About 190

1 | Place 1⅔ cups water and all remaining ingredients in the bread pan in the specified order. Follow the operating instructions for your machine.

2 | Remove the dough from machine, knead briefly and shape into two equal-sized balls. Let rest for 5 minutes. Line a baking sheet with parchment paper. Preheat oven to 400°F. On a floured work surface, roll out dough balls to a 12 inch diameter. Cut each circle into eighths and roll out these triangles to make them slightly larger. Starting with the wide end of the triangle, roll into a crescent. Place on the baking sheet and let rest for 20 minutes. Brush with egg yolk and bake for 20–25 minutes (bottom rack) until golden-brown.

For Company
Party Sun

MAKES 24 ROLLS

- ➤ 2½ tsp salt
  1 tsp sugar
  5 tbs instant mashed potatoes
  ⅛ tsp dry sourdough starter
  5 oz (1 cup) rye flour
  13 oz (3 cups) unbleached all-purpose flour
  1½ tsp instant yeast
  1 tbs bread seasonings (optional)
- ➤ For sprinkling: Poppy seeds, sesame seeds, flaxseeds, oat flakes, pumpkin seeds, sunflower seeds (your choice)
- ➤ Plus:
  Flour for the work surface

🕐 Prep time: 30 minutes

🕐 Resting time: 35 minutes
Setting: Dough cycle

➤ Calories per roll: About 80

1 | Place 2 cups water and all remaining ingredients in the bread pan. Give the machine a little help by scraping the sides with a long-handled plastic spatula until a ball of dough forms.

2 | Remove the dough from the machine. On a lightly floured work surface, knead dough briefly. Line a baking sheet with parchment paper. Divide dough into 24 pieces of 1.5 ounces each and round each piece. Moisten the surface of these balls with water and dip in poppy seeds, sesame seeds, flaxseeds, oat flakes, pumpkin seeds and sunflower seeds. Place on the baking sheet, ¼-inch apart, in a circular pattern to form a "sun." Press down slightly on the rolls with your hand. Preheat oven to 400°F.

3 | Let dough "sun" rest for 30 minutes. Before baking, sprinkle with a little water, then bake for 20–25 minutes (middle rack).

For Company
German Breadsticks

MAKES 9 BREADSTICKS

- ➤ 2 tsp salt
  ⅛ tsp dry sourdough starter
  2 tbs olive oil
  19 oz (4½ cups) unbleached all-purpose flour
  1½ tsp instant yeast

- ➤ For the topping:
  Coarse pretzel salt and caraway seeds
- ➤ Plus:
  Flour for the work surface

🕐 Prep time: 25 minutes

🕐 Resting time: 25 minutes
Setting: Dough cycle

🕐 Timer: Yes

➤ Calories per breadstick: About 240

1 | Place 2 cups water and all remaining ingredients in the pan in order. Follow the operating instructions for your machine.

2 | Remove dough from the machine and round. Let rest for 5 minutes. Flatten dough into a flatbread measuring 8 x 12 inches. Line baking sheet with parchment paper.

3 | Brush flatbread with water. Using a plastic spatula, cut dough into sticks 12 inches long. Moisten your hands and transfer sticks to baking sheet. Let rest for 20 minutes.

4 | Preheat oven to 400°F. Brush sticks with water and sprinkle with salt and caraway seeds. Bake (middle rack) for 25–30 minutes.

For a Buffet
Turkish Breadsticks

MAKES 16 BREADSTICKS

- ➤ 1½ tsp salt
  ½ cup diced ham
  ¾ cup mixed seeds (sunflower seeds, pumpkin seeds, flaxseeds, sesame seeds, poppy seeds)
  1 tbs rye malt
  2 tbs safflower oil
  13 oz (2½ cups) spelt flour
  5 oz (1 cup) rye flour
  1 cup liquid sourdough starter
  1½ tsp instant yeast
- ➤ For sprinkling: Coarse salt and sesame seeds (optional)
- ➤ Plus:
  Flour for the work surface

- 🕐 Prep time: 25 minutes
- 🕐 Resting time: 30 minutes
  Setting: Dough cycle
- ➤ Calories per breadstick: About 190

1 | Place 1½ cups water and all remaining ingredients in the bread pan in the specified order. Follow the operating instructions for your machine.

2 | Line a baking sheet with parchment paper. On a lightly floured work surface, knead dough briefly. Let dough rest for 5 minutes, then roll into a cylinder 8 x 12 inches. Using a plastic spatula, cut dough into long pieces of 3 ounces each and shape into sticks 10 inches long.

3 | Let dough rest for 25 minutes. Preheat oven to 400°F. Before baking, brush with water and sprinkle with salt and caraway seeds, if desired. Bake in the oven (middle rack) for 20 minutes.

For Gourmets
Milk Rolls

MAKES 10 ROLLS

- ➤ 1½ tsp salt
  1 tbs sugar
  2 tsp rye malt
  3 tbs non-fat dry milk
  3 tbs softened butter (optional)
  16 oz (3¾ cups) unbleached all-purpose flour
  1 tsp instant yeast
- ➤ Plus:
  Flour for the work surface

- 🕐 Prep time: 20 minutes
- 🕐 Resting time: 40 minutes
  Setting: Dough cycle
- ➤ Calories per roll: About 200

1 | Place 1⅔ cups water and all remaining ingredients in the bread pan in the specified order. Follow the operating instructions for your machine.

2 | On a lightly floured work surface, knead dough briefly. Line a baking sheet with parchment paper. Divide dough into 10 pieces of 3 ounces each and round each piece. Place balls on the baking sheet, dust lightly with flour and let rest for 5 minutes. Then flatten slightly and cover with a cloth. Let rest in a warm place for 30 minutes. Preheat oven to 400°F.

3 | Press the handle of a wooden spoon across the middle of each ball, almost going through to the bottom. Spray or brush with water. Bake in the oven (middle rack) for 25 minutes until golden-brown.

- ➤ Delicious with hot chocolate.

For Company
New Year's Rolls

MAKES 11 ROLLS

➤ 1 cup milk
1 tsp salt
2 egg yolks
½ cup (1 stick) softened butter
3 tbs sugar
½ tsp vanilla extract
17 oz (4 cups) pastry flour
1 tsp instant yeast
➤ Plus:
1 egg yolk for brushing on surface
Flour for the work surface

🕒 Prep time: 20 minutes
🕒 Resting time: 25 minutes
   Setting: Dough cycle
➤ Calories per roll: About 280

1 | Place ingredients in the bread pan in the specified order and follow the operating instructions for your machine.

2 | Remove finished dough from the machine and knead briefly. Divide into 11 pieces of 3 ounces each and round each piece. Let rest for 5 minutes, then roll into cylinders 6 inches long. Place the pieces side-by-side and up against one another on a baking sheet lined with parchment paper. Cover with a cloth and let rest for 20 minutes.

3 | Preheat oven to 400°F. Just before baking, brush rolls with egg yolk. Bake in the oven (middle rack) for 20–25 minutes.

➤ These rolls taste fantastic with a little jam and coffee or tea, and they're great snack for children.

Classic
Pizza Dough

SERVES 4

➤ 1 tsp salt
1 tsp sugar
2 tbs olive oil
13 oz (3 cups) unbleached all-purpose flour
2½ tsp instant yeast

🕒 Prep time: 25 minutes
🕒 Resting time: 25 minutes
   Setting: Dough cycle
🕒 Timer: Yes
➤ Calories per serving: About 370

1 | Place 1 cup water and all remaining ingredients in the bread pan in the specified order. Follow the operating instructions for your machine.

2 | Remove the dough from the machine and round. Let rest for 5 minutes. Line a baking sheet with baking paper. Roll out dough to the size of the baking sheet or two individual, round pizzas. Let dough rest for 20 minutes. Preheat oven to 400°F. Pierce dough several times with a fork and pre-bake for 8–10 minutes (middle rack). If you prefer a soft crust, skip pre-baking and go immediately to step 3.

3 | Top dough as desired. Bake in the oven (middle rack or one rack higher) for 20–25 minutes until the cheese melts.

➤ Pizza Topping:
Start by spreading the pizza dough with tomato sauce. Top with your choice of pepperoni, fresh mushrooms, olives, etc. Finish with shredded mozzarella and several drops of olive oil. If you prefer your pizza on the spicy side, sprinkle it with red pepper flakes after baking.

Glossary

Baking dishes

As a baking dish, you can use loaf pans made of glass, tin, cast-iron or aluminum, loaf pans with lids, tin cans (remove bottom with a can opener), baking sheets, clay or ceramic pots, etc. If a dish doesn't have a nonstick coating, you'll have to grease it or line it with parchment paper before using. Fill dishes no more than two-thirds full to leave room for the dough to expand. You don't have to grease the bread machine pan because it has a nonstick coating.

Baking mixes

There are many baking mixes available in stores. Most already contain yeast and salt, so all you have to add is water. Be sure to use only high-quality baking mixes, but also remember that nothing beats a dough you mix yourself. Try it and you'll see!

Baking sheet

Grease the baking sheet, or line it with either parchment paper or a silicone mat so you won't have to grease it.

Baking troubleshooting

If you don't like your results—for example, the bread collapsed or rose too much—the most common reason is that you used too much liquid or too much yeast. If the bread is moist, you may have used too much liquid or not enough flour. Next time, be even more exact about your measurements and weigh everything (including liquid) on a good kitchen scale or modify the recipe.

Crushed wheat malt

Crushed wheat malt enhances the flavor of bread and rolls while giving baked goods a delicious, malty taste. In contrast to rye malt, it doesn't make the crumb darker.

Dough rising basket

If you want the dough to retain its shape while rising and not to flatten out too much in the oven, use a dough rising basket. Dusted with flour, it can mark your bread with a decorative, rustic pattern. A dough rising basket lets you use softer dough, for lighter, larger loaves. Dough rising baskets can be made of rye straw, rattan or food-safe plastic. Rising time in a dough rising basket is normally 30 minutes. If you don't have a basket, you can also use a small, wide wicker basket with a cotton or linen lining. Sprinkle this lining lightly with flour and place the dough in the basket. Remember to remove the loaf from the basket before baking.

Gluten

Unlike almost any other flour (except spelt), wheat flour contains a certain protein, called gluten, that is responsible for its superior baking properties. Gluten gives the dough a sort of structure that holds the gas bubbles produced by the leavening agent (such as yeast). As a result, tiny pores form in the dough to make the crumb lighter. The bread rises higher, is lighter and, consequently, more digestible.

Lecithin

Lecithin is a natural emulsifier. If you add it to bread, especially whole-grain bread, it will make the bread rise better, will make it lighter and larger, and will help it stay fresh longer. The bread's crumb will be soft and tender.

Measuring flour

The most accurate and therefore preferred way of measuring flour is with a scale. Volume measuring can vary substantially. Always use a scale when possible. When measuring by volume, always sift your flour first. For the recipes in this book, 1 cup equals 4.5 ounces sifted unbleached all-purpose flour. Both weight and volume measurements are included in these recipes.

Rye malt

Rye malt is a dark roasted malt that enhances the flavor of bread and turns the crumb a darker color.

Tap test

When you bake bread in the oven, you can use the tap test to determine whether it's done. When the baking time is up, remove the bread from the oven using oven mitts, turn it out of the pan and tap the bottom with your knuckle. If it makes a dull thud, the bread is still too moist. Bake it for about 10 more minutes. If it makes a hollow sound, the bread is ready to be cooled on a rack.

Using this Index

To help you find recipes containing certain ingredients more quickly, this index also lists favorite ingredients (such as **spelt flour** or **sunflower seeds**) in **bold type**, followed by the corresponding recipes.

The Author

Ellen A. Harich lives near Munich with her husband and two Golden Retrievers. In addition to hunting, dog training, amateur radio and quilting, she is a passionate baker of bread. She would like to thank all her taste testers who tested and evaluated her bread and helped her to improve it.

The Photographer

After completing his studies at a photography school in Germany, **Michael Brauner** worked as an assistant to renowned photographers in Europe before striking out on his own in 1984. His unique, atmospheric style is valued highly everywhere, as much in advertising firms as by noted publishers. In his studio in Germany, he takes photos that bring to life many of the recipes in this and other cookbooks.

Photo Credits

All photos by Michael Brauner, Karlsruhe

Published originally under the title Brotbackautomat: jederzeit frisches Brot © 2004 Gräfe und Unzer Verlag GmbH, Munich. English translation for the U.S. market © 2006, Silverback Books, Inc.

Program director: Doris Birk
Managing editor: Birgit Rademacker, Lisa M. Tooker (US)
Translator: Christie Tam (US)
Editor: Stefanie Poziombka, Rebecca Friend (US)
Reader: Bettina Bartz
Layout, typography and cover design: Independent Medien Design, Munich
Typesetting: Uhl + Massopust, Aalen
Production: Gloria Pall, Patty Holden (US)

ISBN 1-59637-060-2

Enjoy Other Quick & Easy Books

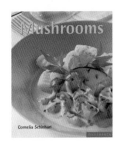

Mushrooms
Cornelia Schinhart

Cooking for One
Christina Kempe

Cocktails & Mixed Drinks
Tanja Dusy & Alessandra Redies

Cooking for Children

Preserves and Canning

Irresistible Fondue
Angelika Illies

Cooking for Two
Cornelia Adam

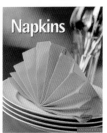

Napkins

Fast Italian
Birgit Procbst

Sushi
Andreas Furtmayr
Classic ideas from Japan and new fusion sushi
Home-made perfectly

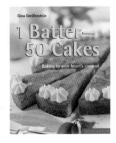

1 Batter— 50 Cakes
Gina Greifenstein
Baking to your heart's content

Cooking in Clay
Healthy Recipes with Great Flavor
Erika Casparek-Türkkan

Coffee and Espresso
Tanja Dusy

Grilling
Crisp, flavorful recipes with specials from the grill that prepare food, from appetizer to dessert, vegetables with sauces and chutneys.

Sauces and Dips

Soups
Classic to Contemporary
Sebastian Dickhaut

Raclette
Claudia Schmidt
New Recipes with Cheese Primer and Party Dips

Antipasti and Tapas
Mediterranean Appetizers
Cornelia Schinhart

1 Pan— 50 Muffins

Salads
Cornelia Adam

Sandwiches
Xenia Burgtof

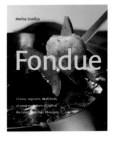

Fondue
Marlisa Szwillus
Cheese, vegetable, meat kinds of meat and other, right at the table, from more than 50 recipes

Christmas Cookies

TOUCH TEST

> Five to ten minutes after starting the cycle, check whether the ingredients are forming an elastic and shiny ball. Using a plastic spatula, carefully push down any ingredients adhering to the sides of the bread pan so that they will be mixed into the dough. If necessary, add flour or water one tablespoon at a time. Listen to the kneading paddle.

Guaranteed Perfect Bread Machine Baking

CLEANING THE BAKING DISH

> Let sticky bits of leftover dough dry in the bread pan, then carefully wipe it out by hand. Use only plain water to clean the dough hooks and bread pan. Use a vacuum cleaner to remove any crumbs or flour that may have fallen beside the bread pan into the machine – but first let the machine cool!

BAKING TIPS

> An atomizer is ideal for spraying bread and rolls with plain water before baking. The moisture gives the bread's exterior more elasticity so it doesn't crack but takes on a beautiful shine. It also helps seeds to stay put.

REMOVING THE DOUGH

> When the dough cycle is finished, sprinkle a little flour onto the surface of the dough. Run a long-handled spatula made of soft plastic all the way around the sides, carefully scraping down to the bottom of the pan. Then just dump out the dough.